To the reader:

Welcome to the DK ELT Graded Rea
different. They explore aspects of the ...ᴗ.ᴗ aᴗund us: its
history, geography, science ... and a lot of other things. And
they show the different ways in which people live now, and
lived in the past.

These DK ELT Graded Readers give you material for
reading for information, and reading for pleasure. You are
using your English to do something real. The illustrations will
help you understand the text, and also help bring the Reader
to life. There is a glossary to help you understand the special
words for this topic. Listen to the cassette or CD as well, and
you can really enter the world of the Olympic Games, the
Titanic, or the Trojan War ... and a lot more. Choose the
topics that interest you, improve your English, and learn
something ... all at the same time.
Enjoy the series!

To the teacher:

This series provides varied reading practice at five levels of
language difficulty, from elementary to FCE level:
BEGINNER
ELEMENTARY A
ELEMENTARY B
INTERMEDIATE
UPPER INTERMEDIATE

The language syllabus has been designed to suit the factual
nature of the series, and includes a wider vocabulary range
than is usual with ELT readers: language linked with
the specific theme of each book is included and
glossed. The language scheme, and ideas for
exploiting the material (including the recorded
material) both in and out of class are
contained in the Teacher's Resource Book.
We hope you and your students enjoy
using this series.

A DORLING KINDERSLEY BOOK

DK www.dk.com

Originally published as Eyewitness Reader
Spacebusters in 1998 and adapted as an
ELT Graded Reader for
Dorling Kindersley by

studio cactus ©

13 SOUTHGATE STREET WINCHESTER HAMPSHIRE SO23 9DZ

Published in Great Britain by
Dorling Kindersley Limited
9 Henrietta Street, London WC2E 8PS

2 4 6 8 10 9 7 5 3 1

Copyright © 2000
Dorling Kindersley Limited, London

A CIP catalogue record for this book is
available from the British Library.

ISBN 0-7513-3182-1

Colour reproduction by Colourscan, Singapore
Printed and bound in China
by L. Rex Printing Co., Ltd
Text film output by Ocean Colour, UK

The publisher would like to thank the following for their
kind permission to reproduce their photographs:
t=top, b=below, l=left, r=right, c=centre,
BC=back cover, FC=front cover

Archive Photos: 3b, 4br, 18tr, 25, 47tr; Corbis-Bettmann:
9br, 22br, 30b; Finley Holiday Film Corporation: 7t;
Frank Spooner Pictures: 47br; Hulton Getty: 2cr, 26l,
36br; Michael Freeman: 17tr, 24br, 34br, 40br; NASA:
1br, 5, 7br, 8t, 15, 16b, 20tr, 21, 28br, 31, 32br, 37c, 44b,
46t, 46b; Rex Features: FC, 4tr, 27br, 29br, 32t, 33r, 45tr,
48br; Robert Opie: 30b; Science Museum/Geoff Dann:
BC; Science Photo Library: 11, 36tr.

Additional photography by James Stevenson.
Jacket credit: NASA

Contents

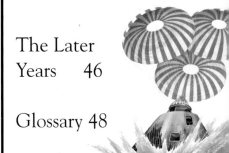

ELT Graded Readers

ELEMENTARY B

RACE TO THE MOON

Written by
Sarah Woolard

Series Editor Susan Holden

London • New York • Delhi • Sydney

Journey to the Moon

Five, four, three, two, one – take-off! Slowly, and with a great roar like an animal, the huge Apollo 11 spacecraft went up off the ground. All the people nearby cheered and shouted as they watched the flames and smoke come out of the bottom of the rocket. Apollo 11 was on its way at last – on its dangerous journey to the Moon.

This was a historic moment. In 1961, President Kennedy made a promise to the people of America, "An American will be on the Moon before the end of the 1960s." Now, it was the summer of 1969 – and Apollo 11 was the last chance to keep that promise. Were these astronauts going to make history?

Outside the spacecraft, many people and journalists were watching and cheering. The photographers were taking pictures for the next day's newspapers. Inside the spacecraft, Commander Neil Armstrong and the other two astronauts could feel their hearts go faster. They all knew that the mission was dangerous. They knew that they had a fifty-fifty chance of getting to the Moon and coming back alive.

It was a dangerous journey, but the astronauts had been trained for this moment. They knew exactly what they had to do. This was work, not a holiday trip!

Take-off, July 16, 1969
The three American astronauts were (from left to right) Neil Armstrong, Michael Collins, and Edwin Aldrin.

Commander Armstrong and the other two astronauts, Aldrin and Collins, had a lot of work to do. Armstrong looked carefully at the instrument panel – everything was looking good. The rocket went faster and faster, and he watched the lights and dials change.

Soon they were travelling at 25,000 miles an hour (40,000 kilometres an hour) – that is thirty times faster than a jet engine. The force now pushed the men back into their seats, and it was very difficult to move. But the astronauts knew this happened at take-off, and they weren't worried. They closed their eyes and waited.

The spacecraft was huge – it was taller than a thirty-storey building. The astronauts sat in a small capsule, but the biggest part of the spacecraft was the huge Saturn V rocket.

This carried all the fuel they needed to get out of the Earth's atmosphere – the air around the surface of the Earth. They needed a lot of fuel to get away from the Earth – but not to travel through space.

After all the fuel was finished, the huge rocket broke away and fell back down to the ground. Then the astronauts continued their journey in the smaller capsule, which was called the Command Module.

The Saturn rocket
After nearly 12 minutes the rocket, now with no fuel, broke away and fell to the ground.

Commander Neil Armstrong

Inside the Command Module, Armstrong turned to talk to Edwin Aldrin. The first part of their journey was finished, and they were out of the Earth's atmosphere. Now it was time to start the second part. "In three days, we will be at the Moon," he said, "It is time to talk about our plans. We have to be sure what to do." Aldrin smiled and nodded.

Aldrin was a happy man. After many years studying space, now he was actually there – and on his way to the Moon! He wanted to walk on the Moon's surface, and to do some scientific experiments there.

Armstrong and Aldrin worked together, and talked about the landing on the Moon. The third astronaut, Michael Collins was feeling hungry, and so he got something to eat. It was strange food! Everything on the spacecraft was weightless – there was no gravity (*see page 22*) – so he couldn't eat normal food.

Normal food didn't stay on the plate in space – it floated up and away. So the astronauts had to eat special space food. This looked a little like baby food, and it was inside a plastic bag. All the food on the spacecraft was dry (there was no water in it), so they could keep it for a long time. Collins picked up a bag, and put some water into it before he ate it. It wasn't like his mother's cooking, but it didn't taste too bad! And you could eat something different for breakfast, lunch and dinner – they had many different kinds of food with them, like beef and chicken.

From time to time, the astronauts thought about "real" food on the Earth. But, for most of the time, food was simply part of the daily routine – it was necessary to stay alive, but it was nothing special!

Space food
Astronauts put water into dried food to make it wet – then no crumbs (or pieces of food) could float around and damage the spacecraft's controls.

The spacecraft travelled very fast towards the Moon, with the Earth behind it, and the three men rested. They would need a lot of energy when they got to the Moon. They had to be wide awake for the dangerous Moon landing, so it was better to sleep now. They had practised sleeping in their strange, weightless state, while they were doing their training. Sleep was an important part of their activity. It was necessary to sleep well to make sure nothing went wrong in the next stage.

Out in space, the heat from the Sun is very, very strong. There was no atmosphere around the spacecraft (like the Earth's atmosphere) to protect it from the Sun's heat. So the capsule turned around and around as it travelled, and this stopped it from getting too hot on one side and catching fire.

Sometimes, when the men looked out of the windows, they could see the Earth. It was beautiful! The Earth was shining brightly, and it looked like a huge ball hanging in space. Everybody was talking about the pictures the astronauts sent back. These pictures changed the way we think about our world.

This moment marked a change from one age to another. In the nineteenth century, the Railway Age had opened up new possibilities. In the twentieth century, the Space Age was about to begin.

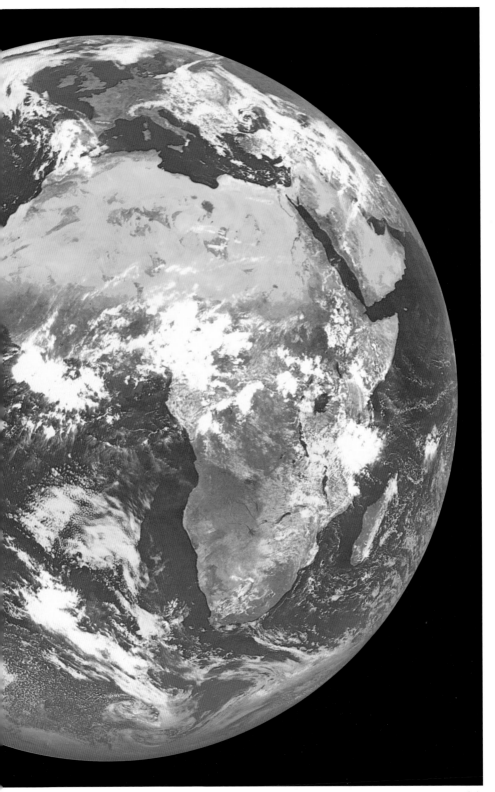

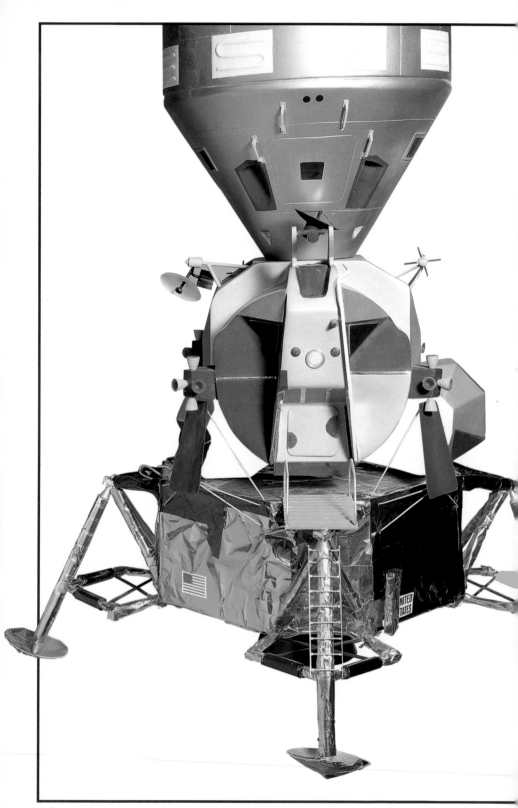

Landing craft under the Command Module.

The astronauts talked more about their plan. They wanted
to land on a part of the Moon called the Sea of Tranquillity.
Of course, it wasn't a real sea, because there is no water on the
Moon. But, from the Earth, it looked a little like a sea, and it
also looked very flat – and a good place for their small craft
to land. So the scientists gave the place this name, and they
programmed the computers on the small spacecraft to land on
this part of the Moon.

Armstrong looked at the clock again – they were on time.
The spacecraft was now circling around the Moon and sending
pictures back to Earth. It was a very important day for television
cameras! This was another "first" in this incredible journey.
Television cameras were going to transmit pictures of the
Moon landing back to Earth. It would be possible for people
sitting at home to watch Armstrong and his colleagues
landing on the Moon. They would see exactly what happened:
a triumph or a disaster!

Then the big moment arrived. It was time for two of the
astronauts to land on the Moon.

Armstrong and Aldrin started to get everything ready for
the next part of their journey. Then they left the Command
Module and went into the small landing craft – this craft
would take them to the Moon. It was small and narrow, and
they climbed inside very carefully. The men called this small
lunar module the "Eagle" (a large bird), but it looked more
like a big spider than a bird!

The lunar module could take two astronauts from the
Command Module down to the surface of the Moon and
then back up again. It had everything the two men
needed to live on the Moon for a short time. And it was the
only craft they had to get off the Moon again.

Michael Collins stayed in the Command Module – his job was to operate the controls there and wait for the other two men to come back. He watched the two astronauts climb into the Eagle and close the door. Then he pressed a button – slowly the small landing craft moved away from the Command Module. Then the Eagle, with the two astronauts inside, moved down towards the Moon's surface. It looked very small. It was on its own!

In the Eagle, Armstrong and Aldrin looked out of the window – soon they could see the lunar surface more clearly – and it was completely different from their ideas!

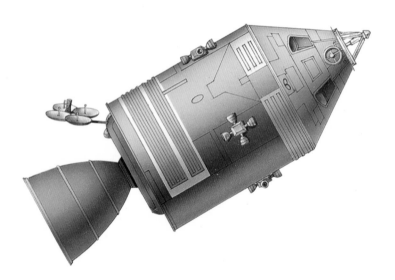

The Sea of Tranquillity looked very different from here. It wasn't really flat, and it looked very difficult to land on. There were many holes (or craters), and a lot of large rocks all around. These rocks were the size of small cars! The two men began to worry – they couldn't see a place to land safely! What were they going to do? They couldn't go back.

The Eagle came closer and closer to the Moon. A computer was steering it and moving it in the right direction – and that was the big problem now!

The scientists on Earth had programmed the computer before take-off. Now the computer couldn't see the dangerous surface in front of them – only the two men could see this out of the window. So the computer continued to steer the Eagle straight on. They were going to crash-land in a huge crater!

Commander Armstrong had to do something – and quickly! He decided to take the controls. Now he was flying the landing craft by himself. This was not in the plan! The plan was for the computer to steer the landing craft. Armstrong and Aldrin should have just been passengers. Armstrong had to think quickly – there wasn't much time.

Steering the landing craft
There were sixteen small rockets around the landing craft. These could make the craft turn right or left, or go up or down to steer it.

"How much fuel is there?" Armstrong asked Aldrin.

"Eight per cent," Aldrin replied.

So there was very little fuel for landing – they only had a few seconds. There was no time to discuss the problem. They had to land quickly – in a place where they could take off again.

Mission Control
Scientists directed the mission from Mission Control in Texas. The person who spoke to the astronauts was called the CapCom.

Then Armstrong saw a good place – it looked flat, and perhaps it was possible to land there. Quickly, he started to steer the craft down. But, as they got nearer to the surface, there was another problem. The rockets on the craft threw up a lot of Moon dust. The dust was everywhere now, and Armstrong could not see where they were going. It was like flying through thick fog.

Then he heard Aldrin say "Contact light." Armstrong looked at the control panel – the light was on. They were down - they were actually on the surface of the Moon! He pressed a button to stop the engine. Then he contacted Mission Control on Earth. "The Eagle has landed," he said. Back at Mission Control in Texas, everybody smiled and cheered.

This was it. Now … what would happen next? For the first time, a human being was going to stand on the Moon.

One Giant Leap

Commander Neil Armstrong wanted to get out immediately and explore the Moon's surface. But he knew it was important to look first at the spaceship's controls. This was the only craft they had – and the only way they could get off the Moon again. The craft had to be ready for take-off. If there was any danger, they wanted to get off the Moon quickly! So he and Aldrin slowly and carefully looked at all the controls. Everything was looking good – they were happy that the craft was ready to go.

Then it was time for them to get ready, and to put on their outside clothes. They had to wear special suits to go outside. The suits were difficult to put on in the small craft, so they helped each other. Then they pulled their enormous overshoes on to their feet, and put their helmets on. The helmets had special visors to prevent the light from the Sun damaging the astronauts' eyes.

They had practised this, too, many times during their training, but it was different in the small landing craft. They knew it was important to get everything right. They had to be sure that the clothes were on properly.

Space clothes
A spacesuit is like a very small spacecraft. It has everything the astronaut needs to live outside the craft, like a radio, oxygen, something to drink, and special pockets to put urine in. It becomes the astronaut's mini-world.

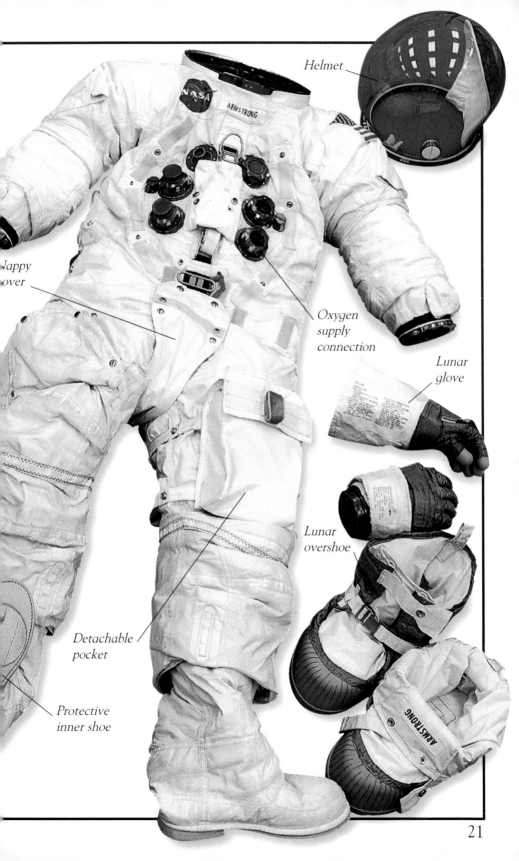

Helmet

NASA ARMSTRONG

Nappy
cover

Oxygen
supply
connection

Lunar
glove

Lunar
overshoe

Detachable
pocket

Protective
inner shoe

ARMSTRONG

It wasn't easy to move around with all those clothes on – and they weren't finished yet, there was more! To breathe on the Moon's surface, each man had to wear a huge backpack with his oxygen supply.

The oxygen backpacks were heavy, but this wasn't a problem, because there is less gravity on the Moon than on the Earth. The men could carry their packs easily.

Finally, when they had put on all their clothes and their oxygen packs, it was time for the astronauts to put on their lunar gloves. Before then, they had needed their hands and fingers free to get everything on. Now, with their gloves on, the spacesuits were complete.

Armstrong and Aldrin pushed a switch on their spacesuits, and they heard a quiet, humming noise – the motors in the backpacks were on. Aldrin felt the oxygen on his face as it went into his helmet. They were finally ready to leave the space module.

So … here was another historic moment – another "first". The astronauts had to go outside the module … to step onto the surface of the Moon.

Back in the Mission Control room, the scientists held their breath. They knew what was going to happen next … or did they?

The force of gravity
This force holds people on the ground. When there is less gravity than on the Earth, people feel lighter and can float.

The cameras in the landing craft were switched on, and they were sending pictures back to Mission Control on the Earth. Everyone there was watching the huge screen, and waiting. Everything was looking good – but it was very quiet in the Mission Control room!

As the scientists on the Earth watched the huge screen, Commander Armstrong pushed the small door open and went outside. This was it! This was the moment they had all been working for. Man … on the Moon.

Armstrong climbed slowly and carefully down the nine steps on the ladder – each step taking him closer to the Moon. He could see the surface clearly now – and everywhere he looked there was dust.

The dust really surprised Armstrong. "It is almost like powder," he said into his radio. And, back on Earth at Mission Control, the scientists listened. Armstrong was a little worried about standing and walking on this dust. Was it deep? Could he walk on it?

Then he stepped off the ladder. Under his feet the ground was hard. Armstrong was happy and very excited – he was the first human being ever to stand on the surface of the Moon. Then he spoke into his radio again – and people all over the world heard his words. "That's one small step for man, one giant leap for mankind."

Those words have become part of history. They are the words that really show that the Space Age had arrived. They show that mankind was entering a new age.

Landing-craft feet
The landing craft had wide feet to stop the legs from sinking into the surface. Gold foil stopped the feet getting too cold.

Neil Armstrong was standing on the Moon! And the first man on the Moon was feeling very excited ... and very nervous. It was a historical moment.

The Moon was very dry. There was very little colour – everything was grey or white. The astronaut lifted his camera and took a photograph: the first photo on the Moon.

A scoop is used to collect rock.

He took a lot of photos: this was his first task. Then he began his second task. He had to get minerals for the scientists back on Earth. The scientists wanted to analyse these minerals to see if the minerals on the Moon were different from those on the Earth.

Armstrong had a big bag for the minerals, and he put some rocks and dust in this. "The scientists will be happy," he thought. "They can do lots of experiments, and become famous like me!"

Then Armstrong closed the bag and said to himself, "OK, I've finished my task, now for some fun! What can I do?" He looked at the bag again. It had a plastic handle, and he had an idea. He took the handle off the bag and threw it away. It was a good throw, and the handle went a long way. The Moon's gravity is very weak, and it couldn't pull the handle down to the surface quickly.

Armstrong was enjoying himself. After the tension of the journey, and the landing, he suddenly felt like a boy again. He waved at Aldrin.

Aldrin was still in the spacecraft. He was watching his friend. "Hey!" he said, "That was a great throw – are you a baseball player? You can be a champion – but only here on the Moon!"

Moon rock
This is a piece of rock from the Moon, brought back by Apollo astronauts. Some Moon rock is 4.6 billion years old.

Aldrin watched from the landing craft. He really wanted to get out of the craft and onto the Moon's surface with his friend. Finally, it was time for him to go!

Like Armstrong before him, he climbed slowly and carefully down the ladder – and then he stepped onto the Moon. Aldrin looked down – everywhere he put his feet there were clear footprints in the dust. This dust was everywhere!

Together, the two men put up the American flag. At first it was difficult to push the flag into the Moon's surface, but then it went in. When it was up, Armstrong and Aldrin stood next to the flag – they felt very proud. Later, they said that this was the best moment in their lives. The scientists back at Mission Control watched the two men, and they also felt proud.

Then Aldrin started to run. Just like Armstrong, he felt all the tension leaving him. Hey, this was fun! The Moon was great! Here they were, two men standing in this great dusty place. And it was the Moon! They were actually standing on the Moon!

He wanted to laugh.

Footprints
There is no wind or rain on the Moon, so the footprints the astronauts made will be there forever.

It was really strange. Aldrin took huge steps while he was running, and he looked like a kangaroo! But he felt he was going very slowly – like watching a film in slow motion. Many people back on Earth were smiling – they couldn't believe their eyes. Here was the serious, historic moment, and the two astronauts were playing like children.

Aldrin stands next to the American flag. They had to make a special flag to stand up by itself, because there is no wind on the Moon.

Armstrong watched Aldrin and laughed, then he tried moving around. They weren't worried about the landing now – they were having a lot of fun!

Suddenly they heard the radio – it was Mission Control. "The President of the United States would like to say a few words to you."

The two astronauts stopped immediately and felt a little embarrassed. They had forgotten that, back on Earth, people were watching them on television. And not just in America – they were watching all over the world.

The Earth and the Moon were linked – by television cameras and, now, by a human voice.

President Richard Nixon spoke to the two astronauts – he had a few words from Earth for the two men.

"All the people on this Earth are truly one," he said. "One in their pride in what you have done."

This moment was an American moment, but also a human, international moment. It belonged to everyone.

Then the astronauts started to get the scientific equipment ready – there was a lot of work to do. First, they put up a special machine that was able to feel any movements on the Moon's surface. To the two men, it looked like there was nothing moving on the Moon – only them. Perhaps the machine could give them more information.

Measuring instrument
This showed that it was 390,000 km (240,000 miles) from the Earth to the Moon. That is more than nine times around the world.

The machine would take measurements and then send the information back to Earth. They also put up an instrument to help scientists measure how far it is from the Earth to the Moon. These measurements were important. They would help the scientists to understand space.

The men worked for two and a half hours, and then they went back to the Eagle to rest. It was hard work trying to put up all the machines and instruments when they were inside their spacesuits. They didn't want to be tired – and careless – when it was time to leave the Moon. They had to take off in the small landing craft and go back to the Command Module to dock with it.

Collins was still in the Command Module, orbiting the Moon and waiting for them. One mistake and they might not dock with the Command Module. The two men in the Eagle would float away into space forever.

In many ways, Collins had the most difficult task. He went to the Moon, but he could not land on it. He had seen his colleagues making history, but he had not stood on the Moon.

Armstrong and Aldrin climbed slowly back up the ladder again and stepped into the landing craft. They closed the small door, and then they looked at each other in surprise – there was moon dust all over their suits! This could be dangerous. Some scientists thought that moon dust would catch fire if it was in oxygen. But the astronauts needed oxygen to breathe inside the Eagle.

They had to turn on the air supply. What was going to happen? They turned it on, and waited nervously. The air went into the small landing craft. But nothing happened – the dust didn't catch fire, and the men smiled.

The two men were tired, and they tried to rest – but it was impossible. They were too excited and nervous, and they were thinking about their next take-off in the Eagle. They also thought about Collins, orbiting the Moon above them. "Where is he? How is he? Will we ever see him again?" they asked themselves.

It was a terrible thought. Without Collins, and the spaceship, they could not return to Earth. They would die on the Moon – alone, in space. Nobody could help them. It was better not to think about such things.

Landing craft engine
The landing craft had one engine for take off from the Moon. It was on for 7 minutes and 45 seconds, and it took the astronauts safely into Moon orbit.

Finally, the time for waiting and resting was finished, and it was time to go – to leave the Moon and go back to Earth. Aldrin pressed the button to start the engine. They heard the noise of the engine and looked out of the window as moon-dust flew all around them again. Then they were off – leaving the legs of the landing craft on the Moon!

Man had been to the Moon – and had left the first piece of human rubbish there!

The landing craft leaves its legs on the Moon at take-off.

Going Home

Collins was sitting in the Command Module, orbiting the Moon. For half of each orbit he was in contact with Mission Control on Earth. But, for the other half, he was on the dark side of the Moon – the side always turned away from the sun. In this half of his orbit, he was alone – no radio signals from Earth could get to him. Everything was silent. Perhaps Collins was more alone than any other human being.

All the time, he was thinking about the landing craft. He was worried about Armstrong and Aldrin down on the Moon's surface. "What will happen if they can't take off?" he thought. "Perhaps there will be a problem with the landing craft, and it won't be able to dock with the Command Module again. If one of these things happens, I will have to go back to Earth alone. Armstrong and Aldrin will die in space."

It was a very difficult and worrying time. Collins waited, and watched his control panel. All he could do was follow the instructions from the training course. He had to continue to wait, and he had to follow the agreed course and to be in the agreed places for the agreed times.

It seemed a very long time.

The Command Module orbits the Moon.

Then, suddenly, Collins saw the landing craft through his window – it was looking good and it was coming towards him. He took the controls and steered the Command Module carefully towards the Eagle.

Slowly, he got the two crafts in line – they were ready to dock. The spacecrafts were very close now – in fact they were almost touching – and this was the most dangerous part. One mistake and the two men in the small landing craft were dead! Again, they had all practised for this moment many, many times in their training back on Earth. But the real thing was different. They felt different. There were no second chances. Time was going very slowly now, and, to the three astronauts, seconds felt like hours.

Armstrong and Aldrin forgot all about the excitement and fun on the Moon – they thought only about docking with the Command Module.

Then they heard a noise, and another, as the two metal doors of the spacecrafts came together. The landing craft was now safely docked with the Command Module. The three men breathed easily again!

Quickly, but carefully, Armstrong and Aldrin climbed back into the Command Module. Collins smiled – everyone was going back to Earth together.

They had done it! It was a success! All the training had prepared them well. The scientists would be pleased. They, too, were part of this successful moon-landing team.

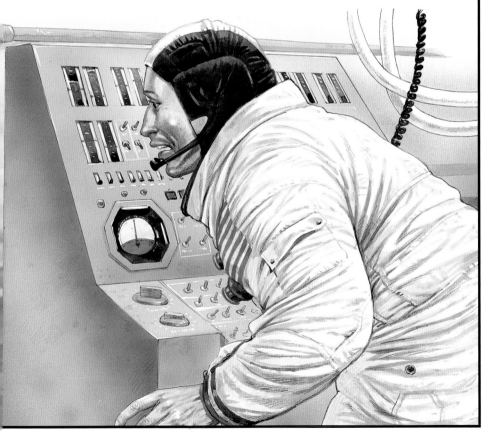

The journey from the Moon back to the Earth took three days, and the astronauts slept for some of this time. While they were sleeping, the force of the Earth's gravity pulled the spacecraft back home.

After three days, the Command Module entered the Earth's atmosphere. Immediately, the outside of the spacecraft started to get hotter and hotter – soon, it was twenty-five times hotter than the oven in your kitchen! This was the final, dangerous part of the journey.

The spacecraft had a special heat shield on the outside, and this stopped it catching fire, or getting too hot. But the astronauts were worried when they looked out of the windows. They saw fire, and pieces of the heat shield come off and fly away. Perhaps the shield wasn't strong enough?

The astronauts and the scientists held their breath. Surely, after the fantastic success of the trip, it couldn't go wrong right at the end? Surely the shield would be strong enough. But would it? The fire was getting brighter and brighter, and more and more pieces of the shield were flying off. Was this the end, after all?

Heat shield
The metals on the spacecraft were very light. They got very hot. So the craft had a special heat shield on top. When it was very hot, the shield caught fire, and the craft stayed cool.

Then there was a loud "Crack!" It was the noise of the small parachutes (called the drogues) opening above them. The astronauts breathed more easily now – the equipment on the outside of the spacecraft was working. The drogues helped to steer the craft so that it came down to Earth safely and in a straight line.

"Whoosh!" There was another strange noise, and air came into the Command Module. A special small window opened up, and soon the air inside the craft was the same as the air outside. It smelt like home!

Then there was another loud noise – this time it was the big parachutes. Armstrong could see them opening above the craft. Now they were floating slowly down. Finally they landed with a loud "Splash!" in the water - they were in the Pacific Ocean. For the first time, the scientists at Mission control could breathe easily again.

They were back on Earth! The mission was a success! They had been to the Moon and walked on it. Now, here they were, safely back home on Earth. After all the planning and training, they had done something new, and it was a success.

It was a very emotional moment.

Everyone smiled, shouted, and cheered loudly in the Mission Control room – the three astronauts were home safely. Special boats were waiting in the ocean. They watched the spacecraft hit the water, and in a few minutes they were beside the craft.

The three men were looking good, but everyone had to be careful at this time. Perhaps there were germs from the Moon on the men or the craft.

Some swimmers from the boats threw special suits to the astronauts, and Armstrong, Aldrin, and Collins put them on. The suits stopped any germs from getting out. But they were not as heavy or uncomfortable as the spacesuits!

Soon they were out of the water and back on land. But it wasn't time to go home yet. The astronauts couldn't speak to anyone or touch anyone. First, the doctors had to examine them and see if they were OK. So they went to a special laboratory where doctors worked with them for about two weeks. President Nixon was there to welcome them home – and to say congratulations and thank-you from the American people.

The laboratory was for the astronauts and their doctors. It was a small room, and not very comfortable. But some of the scientists were not careful enough. They were too excited when they saw the bag of minerals that Armstrong brought back.

They forgot about the possible dangers, and they touched the Moon rocks by accident. So now they had to go into the laboratory with the astronauts.

Then, one hot evening, the doctors said that the astronauts were all in good health – they could go outside. At last, the three men were able to go home to see their wives and their children.

The mission was really over.

The Later Years

After Apollo 11, there were five more Apollo missions to the Moon. Each mission sent a craft to try to land on a different part of the Moon. But one of the later missions had problems, and the astronauts had to come home. That mission was Apollo 13. Now you can see a film of the story.

Scientists made new instruments and equipment to get information from the Moon's surface and send it back to Earth. Some of the astronauts on these missions drove along the surface of the Moon in a kind of car. It was called the Lunar Rover, and it was quite small and battery-powered. In all six missions to the Moon, Apollo astronauts brought back more than 380kg (830 pounds) of Moon rock.

After Apollo 11, Neil Armstrong was a director of the Space Agency in Washington, D.C. When he stopped working, he had his own farm in Ohio.

In 1981, a new kind of spacecraft took off - it was called the Space Shuttle. The big rockets on the Apollo missions were very expensive, and you could only use them once. But the Shuttle can fly many times, on many different missions.

The Shuttle is big enough to carry a lot of scientific equipment into space. Scientists can do many experiments there that are impossible on Earth.

Lunar Rover

The astronauts in the Space Shuttle have taken a lot of scientific experiments and equipment into space. They have also repaired broken equipment in space. For example, some astronauts repaired the huge Hubble Space Telescope. This telescope can give us very interesting – and surprising – pictures of space.

The Shuttle can also take astronauts to space stations that orbit the Earth. Some astronauts have lived in these space stations for many months. They have found out how long humans can live in space. The scientists back on Earth have tested the results of these experiments.

Scientists have sent satellites from the Earth into the Earth's orbit and to many of the planets around us. Satellites have travelled right to the end of our solar system.

What will the next step be?

Edwin Aldrin became a space engineer, designing spacecraft and planning future missions. He also raises money and support for space research.

Michael Collins became director of the National Air and Space Museum, Washington, D.C. It is said to be the world's most exciting museum.

Glossary

Apollo 11
The name of the spacecraft that took a human to walk on the Moon for the first time.

astronauts
Men and women who travel in space, and fly spacecrafts.

atmosphere
The air and other gases that go around the Earth and other planets.

CapCom
The person at Mission Control who talks to the astronauts when they are in space. CapCom is short for Capsule Communicator.

Command Module
The part of the spacecraft where the astronauts lived and worked while they were travelling from the Earth to the Moon.

docking
The joining together of two spacecrafts while they are in space.

drogues
Three small parachutes that helped to keep the spacecraft in a straight line as it fell back to Earth.

gravity
The force that pulls thing towards the ground and holds then there.

heat shield
A special cover on the outside of the Command Module to protect it from high temperatures. The shield kept the craft cool when it came back into the Earth's atmosphere.

laboratory
A room or building where scientists study and do experiments.

landing craft
The smaller spacecraft that the astronauts used to land on the Moon.

Mission Control
A place in Houston, Texas, U.S.A., that is the control centre for space missions. The scientists here direct and control the flights, and talk to the astronauts.

orbit
The journey around a planet (like the Earth or the Moon).

parachute
The thing that makes you fall through the air slowly when you jump out of an aeroplane.

satellite
A machine that is made to orbit the Earth – often used to send messages quickly.

space
The huge area around us that contains all the planets and stars.

spacecraft
Any vehicle that is designed to travel in space.

solar system
The planets around a particular sun. (Our solar system has nine planets)

space shuttle
A spacecraft that can be used again and again to travel into space.